ORANGE
JOURNAL

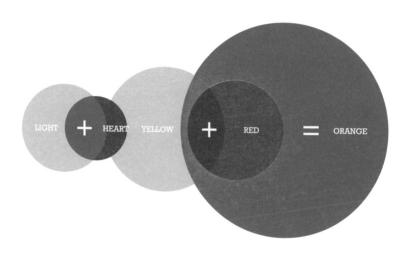

LIGHT + HEART YELLOW + RED = ORANGE

ORANGE ESSENTIALS

FIVE PRIORITIES FOR BUILDING FAITH
IN THE NEXT GENERATION

REGGIE JOINER

ORANGE ESSENTIALS
Published by Orange
A division of The reThink Group, Inc.
5870 Charlotte Lane, Suite 300
Cumming, GA 30040 U.S.A.

The Orange logo is a registered trademark of The reThink Group, Inc.

All Scripture quotations, unless otherwise noted, are taken from the *Holy Bible, New International Version®. NIV®.* Copyright © 1973, 1978, 1984 by International Bible Society. Used by permission of Zondervan.

Other Orange products are available online and direct from the publisher. Visit our website at www.WhatIsOrange.org for more resources like these.

ISBN: 978-0-9854116-1-9

©2012 Reggie Joiner
©2012 The reThink Group, Inc.

Author: Reggie Joiner
The reThink Group Editing Team: Mike Jeffries,
Brad Scholle, Karen Wilson
Design: Ryan Boon & FiveStone

Printed in the United States of America
First Edition 2012

2 3 4 5 6 7 8 9 10 11

10/21/13

YOU ARE THE CHAMPIONS OF FAMILY

YOU ARE THE ADVOCATES FOR THE CHURCH

But most importantly…

You are the MESSENGERS of God

ILLUMINATING | LOVING | DEMONSTRATING

His story of redemption to sons and daughters

Use this book as a tool to

DREAM | CREATE | RECORD

any ideas that will help you have greater influence with the

next generation.

Reggie Joiner

Author, *Think Orange*

www.rethinkgroup.org

EVE RY
GEN

Generations come and go,
but they are all connected . . .

As different as each generation seems to be,
every generation shares . . .

similar history,
common desires,
universal values,
a connected story

History really does repeat itself even though
styles change,
cultures morph,
and the message of truth evolves.

ERA
TION

WHEN A GENERATION CONNECTS TO A BIGGER STORY, THEY ARE
BUILDING ON FOUNDATIONS THAT HAVE ALREADY BEEN LAID.

Every generation needs a
bigger story.

EVERY GENERATION NEEDS TO

MAKE ITS OWN MUSIC
even if the chords are the same;

RAISE ITS OWN VOICE
without compromising what's true;

CELEBRATE ITS OWN FAITH
or it will never become personal.

"Think not forever of yourselves, O Chiefs, nor of your own generation. Think of continuing generations of our families, think of our grandchildren and of those yet unborn, whose faces are coming from beneath the ground."

T.S. ELIOT

"Each generation goes further than the generation preceding it because it stands on the shoulders of that generation. You will have opportunities beyond anything we've ever known."

RONALD REAGAN

"The next generation's product almost never comes from the present generation." Focus – Al Ries

EVERY GENERATION HAS TWO CRITICAL RESPONSIBILITIES:

1 To leverage the efforts and ideas of the generation that came before it

2 To fuel the innovations and faith of the generation that is coming behind it

Every generation needs to

REDISCOVER the art of *strategy*

RESTYLE the presentation of *truth*

RECAPTURE the story of *family*

RESHAPE the value of *community*

REVIVE the potential of its *influence*

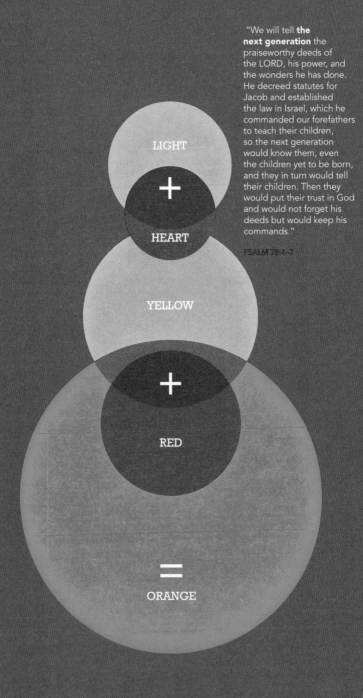

LIGHT

+

HEART

YELLOW

+

RED

=

ORANGE

"We will tell **the next generation** the praiseworthy deeds of the LORD, his power, and the wonders he has done. He decreed statutes for Jacob and established the law in Israel, which he commanded our forefathers to teach their children, so the next generation would know them, even the children yet to be born, and they in turn would tell their children. Then they would put their trust in God and would not forget his deeds but would keep his commands."

PSALM 78:4–7

TWO COMBINED INFLUENCES MAKE A GREATER IMPACT THAN JUST TWO INFLUENCES.

They are both primary influences designed by God for a purpose, and when they work together, they are orange. Both the church and the family are systems comprised of imperfect people that's why God desires to use them as a platform to tell His story of restoration and redemption to the world.

WHAT WOULD HAPPEN IF ...

... churches started believing in the potential of the family to influence their own kids?

... families started believing in the potential of the church to influence their sons and daughters?

Better yet, what if both churches and families started believing in the potential of combining their influences to accomplish the same mission?

The following statements clarify the primary issues most of us agree on, establishing a point of reference for why we believe it is important to think Orange:

* Nothing is more important than someone's relationship with God.

* No one has more potential to influence a child's relationship with God than a parent.

* No one has more potential to influence the parent than the church.

* The church's potential to influence a child dramatically increases when it partners with a parent.

* The parent's potential to influence a child dramatically increases when that parent partners with the church.

If you agree with these thoughts, then I hope you're ready to start a conversation with some of us who think Orange. You can draw your own conclusions and make your own applications as long as, in the end, you are fighting for the destiny of every generation ... because you believe in the potential of the church and the family working together.

Every generation needs the church and family to work together.

There are **8760** hours in a year

The average **PARENT** has 3000 hours in a given year to influence a life.

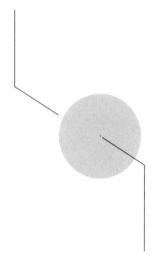

The average **CHURCH** only has **40** hours in a given year to influence a life.

*See **Think Orange**, chapter 4 for more detail on the 3,000/40 principle.*

THE TWO INFLUENCES

There are two powerful influences on the planet:

the church
and the **home**.

They both exist because God initiated them.

They both exist because God desires to use them to demonstrate His plan of redemption and restoration.

If they work together, they can potentially make a greater impact than if they work alone.

THEY NEED EACH OTHER.

Too much is at stake for either one to fail.

Their primary task is to build God's kingdom in the hearts of men and women, sons and daughters.

What's really at stake when the church and the family don't think Orange? There are a number of consequences of isolated red and yellow thinking. Here are some difficulties we see when the church and the family are not advancing the same strategy:

- The church forfeits its potential to have greater influence on kids' and students' lives.

- Churches miss critical opportunities to meet the needs of unchurched parents in their communities.

- Communities continue to perceive the church as institutional, insulated, and irrelevant.

- The church is characterized by superficial relationships.

- Productions or programs are positioned as the answer.

- Parents and leaders will never teach the same truths in a synchronized effort.

- Parents avoid or abdicate to the church the responsibility to be spiritual leaders.

Regardless of your model or style of church, there are some key principles that are critical to helping you create a culture that will think Orange.

FIVE ORANGE ESSENTIALS

Your ability to synchronize the church and the family is intricately connected to how you …

… meet and work together as leaders.

… craft and present truth.

… enlist parents to actively participate.

… recruit leaders to mentor or coach.

… mobilize kids and teenagers to serve.

These issues have an interdependent relationship. Collectively they provide a core framework for combining the influence of the home and church. During the rest of the book we will explore what we consider to be the Five Essentials of Orange.

You can sum it up in one sentence:

Design a strategy that combines family with the faith community to demonstrate the message of God's story, in order to influence the next generation.

DESIGN A ST

THAT COMB

WITH

COMMUNIT

TO   DE

THE

GOD'S STO

INFLUENCE

GENERATIO

EVERY GENERATION NEEDS TO
REDISCOVER the art of strategy

RATEGY

NES FAMILY
THE FAITH
IN ORDER
MONSTRATE
ESSAGE OF
Y TO
THE NEXT
N.

—

INTEGRATE STRATEGY

Align leaders and parents to lead with
the same end in mind

MOST PEOPLE ARE SMART ENOUGH TO HAVE A MISSION.

But really smart leaders realize how important it is to implement a strategy.

NIKE
Crush Reebok.

WAL-MART
Give ordinary folk the chance to buy the same thing as rich people.

WALT DISNEY
Make people happy.

MERCK
Preserve and improve human life.

"ONE" CAMPAIGN
Help make poverty history.

EBAY
Provide a global trading platform where practically anyone can trade practically anything.

TWITTER
A service for friends, family, and co-workers to communicate and stay connected through the exchange of quick, frequent answers to one simple question: What are you doing?

It's the effectiveness of your strategy, not the scope of your mission, that ultimately determines your success.

*From **Think Orange**, page 115*

TRAFFIC CONES

A lot of research has been done to determine why traffic cones should be orange. There's even a Manual on Uniform Traffic Control Devices. It's really amazing how a few pounds of orange thermoplastic and rubber can control the direction of a two-ton car. Hundreds of automobiles are guided every day by the strategic placement of those orange cones.

IT'S ABOUT LEADERSHIP

As a church leader, you have been put in a position to lead families in a specific direction, and it's probably a good idea to spend some time figuring out where you want to lead them. Whether you like it or not, a few misplaced parking cones can confuse a lot of people and lead to some nasty wrecks. You need to make sure that everyone who leads with you is leading in the same direction. Nothing can cause havoc like multiple parking cones scattered across the pavement by independent leaders pointing people in different directions. Frequent communication between all those in charge is essential to avoid potential collisions. If we are going to be effective at creating synergy, we have to sometimes think like the guys who wear orange and know how to handle those orange traffic cones. They have embraced a couple of basic principles:

1. Traffic cones exist primarily to show people where they should go.

2. Traffic cones were designed to work together to have greater influence.

[strategy]

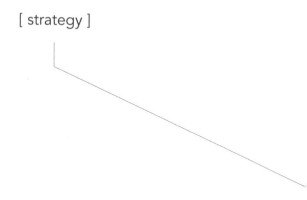

A strategy is a plan of action with an end in mind.

That means you have identified what you want something (or someone) to be, and you have used your creativity and intellect to devise a way to get it there. You have figured out where to place the cones so you can lead people where you want them to be.

INTEGRATE

WHEN WE USE THE PHRASE
INTEGRATE STRATEGY, WE ARE
SUGGESTING THAT YOUR PLAN OF
ACTION SHOULD SYNCHRONIZE
WITH THAT OF OTHERS. IT IMPLIES
YOU ARE COMBINING MULTIPLE
INFLUENCES, PRIMARILY THOSE IN
THE HOME AND CHURCH, WORKING
OFF THE SAME PAGE FOR THE
SAKE OF WHAT YOU WANT TO
ACCOMPLISH IN THE HEARTS OF
THE NEXT GENERATION.

AN INTEGRATED STRATEGY
MEANS THAT LEADERS AND
PARENTS ARE LEADING WITH THE
SAME END IN MIND.

*Read about the lessons we can learn from Nehemiah
on integrating leaders and parents around a common strategy in chapter 6 of* **Think Orange**.

ACTIVITY

CREATE A DREAM TEAM

Who would you want around a table to help you get where you want to go in your ministry or your church? Anybody on the planet is an option. List the unique contribution these people would make to your team.

Name	Contribution

INTERESTING FACTS ABOUT TRAFFIC CONES

The inventor of traffic cones, Charles P. Ruda-baker, came up with the idea when he saw soccer players using class dunce caps as markers on their playing field.

Even though traffic cone manufacturers boast their cones are resilient, standing up to heat, frost, and car tires, local agencies have to replace a number of them each year. However, this is primarily due to people cone-napping them.

A FEW
ORANGE
STRATEGISTS

RONALD REAGAN

When Ronald Reagan was running for President, Nancy Reagan started a tradition many politicians still practice. She would roll a good-luck orange down the aisle of the campaign plane (and later Air Force One) as soon as it took off.

CLIFFORD COOPER

In 1969, young rock hopeful Clifford Cooper built his own guitar amps using tube technology and basic wooden boxes covered with orange vinyl. When his ironically-named band (The Millionaires) went broke, Cooper put the amps in the window of the practice studio to sell for extra cash. Today, artists like U2, Alanis Morissette, Madonna, and Kid Rock still use Orange Amps. (Even the Blue Man Group uses Orange!)

HOWARD DEERING JOHNSON

Ice cream entrepreneur Howard Deering Johnson decided to open a chain of restaurants in the 1930s with a friendly feel for travelers on the new Interstate Highway system. The orange-roofed Cape Cod-style houses became national landmarks for those looking for a good meal and a safe place along the lonely road.

"In strategy it is important to see distant things as if they were close and to take a distanced view of close things."

Miyamoto Musashi, 1584-1645, legendary Japanese swordsman

"The essence of strategy is choosing what not to do."

Michael Porter, Harvard Business School

"Just because you have always done it that way doesn't mean that it is not incredibly stupid."

Unknown

ACTIVITY

CREATE A STOP DOING LIST

What are some things you should stop doing so you can do some other things better? They are those things you have to manufacture energy to keep going. Intuitively, you know they are keeping something else from working. Be courageous. Just write them down and put a date down that you want them to stop.

Activity   Date

WE BELIEVE THAT WE'RE ON THE FACE OF THE EARTH TO MAKE GREAT PRODUCTS.

WE BELIEVE IN THE SIMPLE, NOT THE COMPLEX.

WE BELIEVE THAT WE NEED TO OWN AND CONTROL THE PRIMARY TECH-NOLOGIES BEHIND THE PRODUCTS WE MAKE.

WE BELIEVE IN SAYING NO TO THOU-SANDS OF PROJECTS SO THAT WE CAN REALLY FOCUS ON THE FEW THAT ARE TRULY IMPORTANT AND MEANINGFUL TO US.

WE BELIEVE IN DEEP COLLABORATION AND CROSS-POLLINATION OF OUR GROUPS, WHICH ALLOW US TO INNOVATE IN A WAY THAT OTHERS CANNOT.

WE DON'T SETTLE FOR ANYTHING LESS THAN EXCELLENCE IN EVERY GROUP IN THE COMPANY, AND WE HAVE THE SELF-HONESTY TO ADMIT WHEN WE'RE WRONG AND THE COURAGE TO CHANGE.

WE PARTICIPATE ONLY IN MARKETS WHERE WE CAN MAKE A SIGNIFICANT CONTRIBUTION.

SUMMARY OF TIM COOK, CEO OF APPLE, REGARDING APPLE'S BUSINESS PHILOSOPHY

INTEGRATE
STRATEGY

Align leaders and parents to
lead with the same end in mind

DO YOU HAVE A PLAN THAT WORKS?

DESIGN A S
THAT COMB
WITH
COMMUNIT
TO
THE
DE
GOD'S STO
INFLUENCE
GENERATIO

EVERY GENERATION NEEDS TO
RESTYLE the presentation
of their message

RATEGY
NES FAMILY
THE FAITH
IN ORDER
MONSTRATE
IESSAGE OF
Y
TO
THE NEXT
.

—

REFINE THE MESSAGE

Craft core truths into engaging, relevant, and memorable experiences

CARROTS

Up until the 16ᵗʰ Century, carrots were grown in a variety of hues: red, black, yellow, purple, and even white. There were no orange carrots until the 17ᵗʰ Century when some Dutch growers began feeling patriotic. In honor of their king, William of Orange, they married some yellow and red carrots to produce our modern-day orange carrots. I imagine there must have been some orange carrot skeptics in the beginning. They were probably overheard saying things like:

"These can't be true carrots,"

OR

"Carrots aren't supposed to look like that,"

OR

"Those are not the kind of carrots my parents ate."

Nevertheless, the color of carrots changed forever. But here's an important point: CHANGING THE COLOR OF CARROTS DID NOT ALTER THE FUNDAMENTAL NATURE OF THE CARROT. In other words, orange carrots were just as nutritious as black carrots. The only real difference between the two was that more people were willing to eat orange carrots than black ones.

It's not *what you say*,
it's how you say *what you say*.

If you knew
more kids
and students
would engage
in what you
teach if you
packaged it
differently,
would you?

Would you color it Orange if more kids would listen? Before you start using phrases like "watering down the truth" or "not deep enough," just remember you can change the color of something without compromising its nature. It doesn't mean you weaken your message just because you focus on what your audience needs. The principle is clear. If you want more people to eat carrots, then change the color. If you want more students to listen to what is true, change how you present it.

- It's okay to communicate in a way that's fun.

- It's smart to use language they can understand.

- It's responsible to believe that how you teach the truth may determine whether or not it's actually heard.

> "Making the simple complicated is commonplace; making the complicated simple, awesomely simple, that's creativity."
>
> CHARLES MINGUS

SAY LESS
MORE OFTEN
SO EVERYONE
WILL KNOW
WHAT REALLY
MATTERS.

1
SAY LESS
Be selective about WHAT you say.

2
MORE OFTEN
Be strategic about HOW OFTEN you say it.

3
SO EVERYONE WILL KNOW
Be intentional about WHO else says it.

4
WHAT REALLY MATTERS
Be creative about HOW you say it

REFINE
MESSAGE

Craft core truths into engaging, relevant, and memorable experiences

LESS IS MORE

"The ability to simplify means to eliminate the unnecessary so that the necessary may speak."

Hans Hofmann

600,585
words in the Old Testament

THERE ARE ABOUT ...
800,000 words in the Bible

But only **25,000** of Jesus' words were actually recorded.

Those words changed the world then.

They are still changing the world now.

So you can say less and still make an impact.

180,552
words in the New Testament

Jesus boiled everything down to what is most important.

"'Love the Lord your God with all your heart and with all your soul and with all your mind. ' This is the first and greatest commandment. And the second is like it: 'Love your neighbor as yourself.'"
Matthew 22:37–39

RELEVANCE

I haven't run into many non-Christians who don't go to church because it's too relevant. I hear descriptions like "boring," "old," "can't fit in," and "judgmental," but not the word "relevant." Instead of running into churches that are too relevant, I tend to see the fallout from people who claim the church is irrelevant.

Churches have a bad habit of sacrificing the potential that exists in timeless, life-changing truths because they fail to communicate those truths in a relevant or helpful way. We are notorious for answering questions they just are not asking. It's like …

… giving a drink of water to someone who is cold.

… handing jumper cables to a man with a flat tire.

… telling a story to someone who is bleeding.

Whether we are church leaders, parents, or teachers (and whether we are working with preschoolers, kids, or teenagers), we must all learn to ask this question: Is this really helpful or relevant to their season of life?

From **Think Orange**, page 141

Ron Crossland and Boyd Clarke write in The Leader's Voice that leaders consistently make

4
FATAL ASSUMPTIONS when they communicate:

The people
UNDERSTAND
what I said.

The people
AGREE
with what I said.

The people
CARE
about what I said.

The people will take
APPROPRIATE ACTION based on what I said.

SYNCHRONIZE

It is important to **refine your message** to a few core principles that help parents and leaders stay focused on the bigger picture. When you use the same terminology to show the foundation of your content from preschool to students, it amplifies the **BIG PICTURE** of what you are trying to say. It helps everyone—staff, leaders, and parents— understand the value of a **COMPREHENSIVE PLAN**.

From *Think Orange*, page 142

THE
POWER
OF WORDS

We live in a media-driven generation in which people grab powerful words and hold on to them. Just check out people's Facebook pages and read their favorite quotes. You don't see a lot of fluffy or wordy sentences that go on forever. You see phrases from poems, punch lines from movies, statements from famous people, and something Jack Bauer said. The cultural world around us is reinventing how it says what it says all the time. Writers will go on strike over intellectual property and millions of dollars will be spent, all because of the power of words. We brand them, sing them, wear them, film them, drive them, graffiti them, buy them, sell them, claim them, and speak them. And if there are any two entities that should work hard to leverage words effectively, they are the church and the home. What we have to say is more important than anything.

*From **Think Orange**, page 143*

ACTIVITY

Collect some quotable statements from your friends'
Facebook or blog pages. Take a look at what they
think is worth remembering.

"I know what you're
thinking. Did he fire six
shots or only five? Well,
to tell you the truth, in
all this excitement, I've
kinda lost track myself.
But being as this is a
.44 Magnum, the most
powerful handgun in
the world, and would
blow your head clean
off, you've got to ask
yourself one question:
Do I feel lucky? Well, do
ya punk?"
Dirty Harry

"I like nonsense; it wakes
up the brain cells."
Dr. Seuss

"Your life is defined by
its opportunities ... even
the ones you miss."
Benjamin Button

"It's only after you've lost
everything that you're
free to do anything."
Fight Club

"Carpe, carpe diem. Seize
the day boys. Make your
lives extraordinary."
Dead Poets Society

WHAT WORDS DO YOU REMEMBER?

DESIGN A S[TORY]
THAT COMB[INES]
WITH
COMMUNIT[Y]
TO   DE[...]
THE
GOD'S STO[RY]
INFLUENCE[...]
GENERATIO[N]

EVERY GENERATION NEEDS TO
RECAPTURE the story of the family

RATEGY

NES FAMILY

THE FAITH

IN ORDER

MONSTRATE

IESSAGE OF

Y   TO

THE   NEXT

N.

—

REACTIVATE THE FAMILY

Enlist parents to act as partners in the spiritual formation of their own children

JACK-O-LANTERNS

Most families love Halloween. Right or wrong, there is something about October 31 that stirs the imagination of children
and engages the hearts of parents.

Watch your neighborhood closely this fall.

Listen to the laughter.

Take a look at the generosity.

Taste the sugar.

Feel the energy.

See the glow in the children's eyes.

Notice the parents walking with their kids.

And observe how families connect with other families.

It seems kind of ... magical.

WHY CAN'T CHURCH BE MORE LIKE THAT?

Why can't the church create the kind of atmosphere for the family that captures their imagination and incites a relational revival in the home? It can, if you **think Orange**. Halloween Orange! No, I am not endorsing anything, just observing. What if you started thinking differently about the family? Better yet, what if you started acting differently toward parents? Has it ever occurred to you that how you relate to parents may influence how you reactivate the family? By "reactivate the family," we simply mean the way you help parents actively participate in the spiritual formation of their own children.

Why is it that so many parents who are coming back to church claim that the church has not really helped them lead their kids spiritually? Maybe it's because the church has been programmed to only think in terms of the color yellow. We don't really know how to partner with parents. Our programming and resources are built around the forty hours we have with kids.

Only one out of five parents who attend church say they have ever been contacted by their church to discuss their responsibility to influence their children spiritually.

INFLUENCING

When parents show up at church, they are often asking silent questions that we must answer, questions they don't even know they're asking. To begin looking at parents through a different filter, imagine that every time a parent walks through the door, he or she is asking you **to do three things**:

PARENTS

1

Give me the plan. Most parents are parenting reactively, yet many of them desire to be proactive. They want a plan that will give them a system of support, consistent influence, and a steady flow of relevant information.

2

Show me how it works. Parents need influence as much as children do, and they desire to be engaged in the process in a way that prompts them to take the best next step.

3

Tell me what to do today. If we are going to truly partner with parents, we have to give them specific instructions or resources to use this week.

SPIRITUAL LEADERSHIP

If you're going to help a parent know how to be a "SPIRITUAL LEADER," then you should consider telling a parent what that phrase actually means. As church leaders, we are notorious for using phrases that have been passed down to us, but we have never stopped to ask what those phrases mean exactly. If you were to send me an e-mail with a clear definition of spiritual leadership, what would it be? Have you ever written one? Church leaders are in a great position to redefine it in terms that are practical and possible. I am convinced that most parents feel inadequate when they hear the term, and as a result they are not sure it's something they can do.

From *Think Orange*, page 90

REACTIVATE
FAMILY

Enlist parents to act as partners
in the spiritual formation of their
own children

How do you measure a
successful partnership
with parents?

THE GOAL IS NOT TO ENGAGE
PARENTS TO DO EVERYTHING,
BUT TO ENGAGE THEM TO DO

SOMETHING MORE.

WHAT IF...

one dad who hasn't been **praying** with his ten-year-old daughter starts praying with her

one mom who hasn't **connected** with her teenage son convinces him she really cares

one family who rarely discusses **spiritual issues** starts talking about God at dinner, even occasionally

anything changes in the rhythm of the home to remind everyone that **God is telling a story** through their family

one son or daughter sees **God at work** in the life of a mom or dad

... IT IS MORE IMPACTING THAN ANY LEADER OR PARENT CAN IMAGINE.

GIVE PARENTS HOPE

Some of you are in a better position to influence families than many parenting experts. Assuming that you believe in the importance of family, you have a decision to make about your approach to parents:

A. You can decide that most parents will probably never change.

B. You can challenge parents to an idealistic and unattainable standard.

OR

C. You can choose to believe that most parents, regardless of their baggage, have the desire and capacity to improve.

Make it your goal to convince parents of the following:

God is at work telling a story of restoration and redemption through your family. Never buy into the myth that you need to become the "right" kind of parent before God can use you in your children's lives. Instead, learn to cooperate with whatever God desires to do in your heart today so your children will have a front row seat to the grace and goodness of God.

*Learn how to keep all kinds of parents engaged in your church's strategy by understanding the Loop of Engagement in chapter 8 of **Think Orange**.*

ACTIVITY

VIP PARENTS

If you had to make a list of parents who would be important to involve in your ministry as leaders, who would they be? It is vital to tap into influential parents to give you feedback and to provide an important voice to other parents.

"What happens at home is more important than what happens at church."

So here's a Parent CUE
Connect to God's Story
Uncover something about life
Experience something together

> IF YOU EVER START FEELING LIKE YOU HAVE THE GOOFIEST, CRAZIEST, MOST DYSFUNCTIONAL FAMILY IN THE WORLD, ALL YOU HAVE TO DO IS GO TO A STATE FAIR. BECAUSE FIVE MINUTES AT THE FAIR, YOU'LL BE GO-ING, 'YOU KNOW, WE'RE ALL RIGHT. WE ARE DANG NEAR ROYALTY.'
>
> Jeff Foxworthy

FAMILY AS A
PRIORITY

"There is no doubt that it is around the family and the home that all the greatest virtues, the most dominating virtues of human society, are created, strengthened and maintained."

Winston Churchill

"If you bungle raising your children, I don't think whatever else you do well matters very much."

Jackie Kennedy

"Your success as family, our success as a society, depends not on what happens in the White House, but on what happens inside your house."

Barbara Bush

"My first job in all honesty is going to continue to be mom-in-chief. Making sure that in this transition, which will be even more of a transition for the girls … that they are settled and that they know they will continue to be the center of our universe."

Michelle Obama

"Our Dad, who read to us nightly, taught us how to score tedious baseball games. He is our father, not the sketch in a paper or part of a skit on TV. Many people will think they know him, but they have no idea how he felt the day you were born, the pride he felt on your first day of school, or how much you both love being his daughters. So here is our most important piece of advice: remember who your dad really is."

Excerpt from Jenna and Barbara Bush's
letter to Sasha & Malia Obama

FAMILY SHAPES US.

FAMILY CONNECTS US.

FAMILY INFLUENCES OUR STORY.

WHO IS SHAPING
YOUR STORY?

DESIGN A S
THAT COME
WITH
COMMUNIT
TO   DE
THE
GOD'S STO
INFLUENCE
GENERATIO

EVERY GENERATION NEEDS TO
RESHAPE the value of community

RATEGY

NES FAMILY

THE FAITH

IN ORDER

MONSTRATE

ESSAGE OF

Y

> "To the world, you may just be somebody. But to somebody, you just might be the world."
>
> UNKNOWN

TO

THE NEXT

N.

ELEVATE COMMUNITY

Connect everyone to a caring leader and a consistent group of peers

BASKETBALL

Many people know that in 1891 Dr. James Naismith invented the game of basketball. Not a lot of people, however, know about the contribution of Tony Hinkle in the late 1950s. Hinkle made it easier for spectators and players to see the ball by making it orange. Today, basketball is the only sport that has an official orange ball.

Any winning team has to meet on a frequent basis to practice plays, learn strategies, and increase personal skills. The (right coach) can make all the difference. The next time you watch a basketball game, focus on the head coach. The coach moves along the sidelines with the players, giving constant instructions. Maybe the most mysterious part of the game is how the players seem to have supersonic laser-focused hearing. They can actually filter out the echoes of the gym floor, the roar of the crowd, and the shouts of their own parents to tune in to (the solitary voice) of the coach.

Every kid needs another adult voice in their life.

LEAD SMALL.

When you lead small we simply make a choice to invest strategically in the lives of a few over time so we can help them build an authentic faith.

1. BE PRESENT
2. CREATE A SAFE PLACE
3. MOVE THEM OUT
4. PARTNER WITH THE PARENTS
5. MAKE IT PERSONAL

The reality is, there comes a time in all children's lives when they seem to care more about what another adult says than they care what their own parents say. That's why it's important to start early in a child's life establishing the right influences.

When we talk about elevating community, we are talking about strategically placing leaders in the lives of our children and teenagers. Growing up in this generation requires some pretty significant relationships. Children and students need the skills to navigate through difficult obstacles and the right voices to give wise direction.

> [
> Everyone needs to be believed in
> by someone, and everyone needs
> to belong somewhere.
>]

If you look back over your own life, you will probably notice that certain individuals stand out over time because of the impact and influence they had in your life. It's the power of significant relationships. When churches embrace this principle, they help parents by meeting the needs of children and teenagers to have older mentors to guide and encourage them in their faith. One of the greatest gifts your church can give its families is a consistent network of leaders and friends who are there to help them win.

ACTIVITY

LOOKING BACK

> "I've learned that something constructive comes from every defeat."
>
> Tom Landry

> "The greatest accomplishment is not in never falling, but in rising again after you fall."
>
> Vince Lombardi

Make a list of the key leaders who coached or inspired you spiritually. Also use this to keep a list of those who you have decided to coach.

1.
2.
3.
4.
5.

"Life is ten percent what happens to you and ninety percent how you respond to it."

Lou Holtz

EVERYONE NEEDS A COACH THAT WILL MOVE THEM PAST THE OBSTACLES... IN FACT, WHETHER OR NOT A STUDENT REMAINS INVOLVED IN A FAITH COMMUNITY IS TIED TO THE NUMBER OF ADULTS WHO INFLUENCE THAT PERSON SPIRITUALLY.

*Read real stories of the influence of other adults in children's and students' lives in chapter 9 of **Think Orange***

ELEVATE
COMMUNITY

Connect everyone to a caring
leader and a consistent group
of peers

In his research, Mike Kelley observed,

"TEENS WHO HAD AT LEAST ONE ADULT FROM CHURCH MAKE A SIGNIFICANT TIME INVESTMENT IN THEIR LIVES ... WERE MORE LIKELY TO KEEP ATTENDING CHURCH. MORE OF THOSE WHO STAYED IN CHURCH BY A MARGIN OF 46 PERCENT TO 28 PERCENT SAID FIVE OR MORE ADULTS AT CHURCH HAD INVESTED TIME WITH THEM PERSONALLY AND SPIRITUALLY."

COMMUNITY MATTERS

"THERE IS ALWAYS SOME KID WHO MAY BE SEEING ME FOR THE FIRST OR LAST TIME, I OWE HIM MY BEST."

Joe DiMaggio

DO SOMETHING CULTURE CAN'T DO

No matter how much the culture tries to mimic community by creating false environments and shallow relationships, the culture can never be a consistent, personal presence in the lives of parents and children. Creating community is something every church can do regardless of size or budget simply by placing another consistent adult in the life of every child and student in your ministry. When this happens, children and students know they have a place where they can have a safe and meaningful spiritual discussion with an adult who cares. When that happens, nothing can compete.

"I MAKE SAM [MY SON] GO [TO CHURCH] BECAUSE THE YOUTH GROUP LEADERS KNOW THINGS I DON'T. THEY KNOW WHAT TEENAGERS ARE LOOKING FOR, AND THEY NEED ADULTS WHO HAVE STAYED ALIVE AND VITAL, ADULTS THEY WOULDN'T MIND GROWING UP TO BE. AND THEY NEED TOTAL ACCEPTANCE OF WHO THEY ARE, FROM ADULTS THEY TRUST, AND TO BE WELCOMED IN WHATEVER CONDITION LIFE HAS LEFT THEM NEEDY, WALLED OFF. THEY WANT GUIDES, ADULTS WHO KNOW HOW TO ACT LIKE ADULTS BUT WITH A KID'S HEART. THEY WANT PEOPLE WHO WILL SIT WITH THEM AND TALK ABOUT THE BIG QUESTIONS, EVEN IF THEY DON'T HAVE THE ANSWERS; ADULTS WHO WON'T CORRECT THEIR FEELINGS OR PRETEND NOT TO BE AFRAID. THEY ARE LOOKING FOR ADVENTURE, EXPERIENCE, PILGRIMAGES, AND THRILLS. AND THEN THEY WANT A HOME THEY CAN RETURN TO, WHERE THINGS ARE STABLE AND WELCOMING."

ANNE LAMOTT

WHO WILL YOU INSPIRE?

DESIGN A S
THAT COMB
WITH
COMMUNIT
TO   DE
THE
GOD'S STO
INFLUENCE
GENERATIO

EVERY GENERATION NEEDS TO
REVIVE the potential of
their influence

RATEGY
NES FAMILY
THE FAITH
IN ORDER
MONSTRATE
ESSAGE OF
Y TO
THE NEXT
.

LEVERAGE INFLUENCE

Consistent opportunities are created for students to experience personal ministry

The heart will gravitate toward whatever offers adventure and significance.

MOUNTAIN CLIMBING

So what do you think would be more exciting—going to classes that teach you about mountain climbing, or actually standing at the summit after a hard climb to get a firsthand look at the view? Imagine sitting for several years and listening to someone describe the adventures related to climbing mountains. How would it affect you if you never really climbed a mountain yourself? Do you think you would be more or less motivated to climb? Here is a profound question. Do think climbers climb just because they have heard about climbing or because one day they started climbing?

Here are a few realities. If you never actually climb …

… you will miss the discovery of personal capacity.

… you will miss the passion of engaging with the mountain.

… you will miss the wonder that comes with seeing the view.

But this is about more than just mountain climbing. The same principles hold true for the kids and teenagers who grow up in our homes and churches. Somehow we believe that if we only talk about the importance of faith and teach them how to show faith, they will automatically grow in their faith. At what point do you think it is appropriate for students to grab some rope and start heading up the side of a mountain? Most churches spend a lot of energy trying to get students to come to programs where they talk about growing as a Christian, but they forget that the way you grow is by experience.

*From **Think Orange**, pages 205-206*

The heart will gravitate toward whatever offers adventure and significance.

The bottom line is that everybody needs to experience something bigger than themselves. Whether we provide them the opportunity to do so or not, they will look for a way to participate in something adventurous.

LEVERAGE INFLUENCE

Consistent opportunities
are created for students to
experience personal ministry

"History will have to record that the greatest tragedy of this period of social transition was not the strident clamor of the bad people, but the appalling silence of the good people."

MARTIN LUTHER KING, JR.

ACTIVITY

DESIGN AN ADVENTURE

Start planning some possible experiences that could capture the imagination of your families, kids, or teenagers. Think of it this way: If you were personally mentoring eight ninth-grade boys or girls for three years, what are at least three things you would do to "experientially" to build their faith?

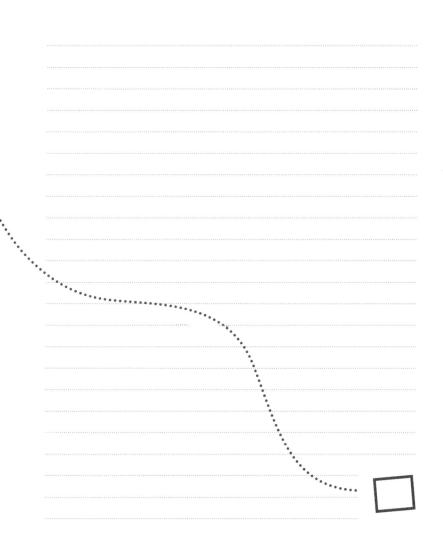

GIVE THEM
AN ADVENTURE

One of the reasons some students are walking away from the church is because they have found something more exciting to walk away to—they have discovered what seems to be a bigger story. When they look back at their church involvement, it was static and non-eventful. They have never experienced the intoxicating kind of faith that comes when they allow God to work through their lives. They didn't have a hands-on encounter with ministry that gave them a personal sense of God's mission. They missed out on the passion that results when you collide with humanity to care for someone in a crisis situation.

When there is nothing dangerous or adventurous about your style of faith, you begin to drift toward other things that seem more interesting and meaningful. Be honest, what does the average teenager in the average church really experience? When do we stretch their faith? When do we push them into ministry situations where they have to depend on God to do something in them and through them? When do we consistently give them opportunities to develop a personal ministry? The average high school teenager can get a job, drive a car, apply to college, and open a bank account, but we very rarely allow them to lead or serve in a ministry inside or outside the church.

What makes us think that students
will do ministry when they leave us
if they never do ministry while
they are with us?

EVERY GENERATION NEEDS TO

SO REMEMBER

rediscover the art of
STRATEGY

recapture the
story of **FAMILY**

restyle the
presentation of
THEIR MESSAGE

reshape the
value of
COMMUNITY

Every generation needs to

revive the
potential of their
INFLUENCE

The potential of the
church and family
combining their efforts
has huge potential
in reaching the next
generation.

ORANGE
THINKING
JUST A DIFFERENT WAY OF LOOKING
AT EVERYTHING YOU DO

ORANGE THINKING IS NOT
EITHER/OR, IT REALLY IS BOTH/AND.

IF YOU ARE THINKING BOTH/AND,
YOU ARE SYNCHRONIZING THE EFFORTS OF THE
CHURCH AND FAMILY
AROUND A MASTER PLAN.

STRATEGY If you are thinking both/and, YOUR KEY STAFF LEADERS ARE BECOMING both specialists AND generalists who will break down silo thinking.

MESSAGE If you are thinking both/and, you are valuing truths THAT ARE CORE and evolving your style to connect with culture.

FAMILY If you are thinking both/and, you are CULTIVATING SPIRITUAL AND MORAL LEADERSHIP in parents who are inside and outside your church.

COMMUNITY If you are thinking both/and, you are TAPPING INTO THE INFLUENCE of the parent and recruiting other adults to build influence with kids and teenagers.

INFLUENCE If you are thinking both/and, you are MOBILIZING VOLUNTEERS to BE the church and they are mobilizing those they are influencing to BE the church.